K. VERMAAK

ESCAPING THE WELL OF SILENCE

THE 30 DAY GUIDE FOR SPEAKERS, LEADERS AND COACHES WHO WANT TO WRITE A BOOK

Escaping the Well of Silence

K Vermaak

Write Learn and Earn

Escaping the Well of Silence

Author: K Vermaak

ISBN (Print): 978-0-7961-1671-0
ISBN (E-book): 978-0-7961-1672-7

Cover Layout: Gregg Davies
Layout and Formatting: Write, Learn and Earn
Chapter Image by: Gordon Johnson from Pixabay
Author Photo: Linda Magennis
Edited by: Jane Mqamelo
Published by: Write Learn and Earn

First Edition: 2024

https://www.writelearnandearn.co.za

Disclaimer

This book is intended to act as a writing prompt for writers to release their creativity.

All characters and other entities appearing in this work are fictitious, and any similarities to actual people and events are purely coincidental.

This book is dedicated to Jann Weeratunga.

Children's Author - Paralympics for Pirates - Polly's Piralympics.
Advocate for kids' books with disabilities as their focus

You were the first author who understood my fears of getting started. Thank you for introducing me to the power of writing prompts and for your ear and kind heart over the years.

Contents

Foreword

I STOOD POISED ABOVE the bin, a thick manuscript in my hand. The voices in my head said, "Why are you doing this to yourself?"

"You don't need to expose your challenges. You can stay hidden. You can drown these words into the well of silence. Then you can retreat back into quiet anonymity. No-one needs to know the anguish of these pages."

Another small voice whispered, barely audible.

I paused.

My hand was shaking. The voice trembled as it caressed my arm.

"Maybe, just maybe, your story can help someone else. Maybe it's not about you anymore".

The whisper broke the well of silence. The words rose from the inky darkness of the blackened water below. Pools of meaning. The choreography of the dancing paragraphs illuminated my past. Words of healing, words of hope, rose from the anguish of the silent well. Words buried for so long.

It was Kim's voice that deepened my identity as a writer. *"Your words matter,"* she said. *"Your message has layers of meaning."*

Now I know that writing has made sense of my entire life.

Did you ever know that you had a book in you? That you had a story to tell. But you did not know where to start?

You know deep down, in the dark wells of your soul, you have a story to tell, whether for family, friends, colleagues or strangers?

This book is as unique as Kim's calling in the world. This is not a book about writing. This is a book about silencing the voices in your head so that the words tumble out of your soul.

If you follow the prompts of the seeds that have been sown, you will know by the end of this immersion that you possess the ability to be a writer.

That you can no longer silence the voices in your soul. The voice of your legacy.

You came here for a reason. You came here to make a difference. Your voice matters.

Write without judgement. Write from the heart.

Just write.

This book is Kim's gift to the world.
Your words are the gift of your soul.
They can no longer be silenced.
The water of your words.

Alison Weihe

Author, Speaker, Coach and Entrepreneur.

Getting Started

"No one is actually dead until the ripples they cause in the world die away."

Terry Pratchett

I DISCOVERED THE VALUE of writing prompts through the 2000 drama 'Finding Forrester', starring Sean Connery and Rob Brown. In one scene, recluse writer William Forrester (played by Sean Connery) places a piece of his work in front of aspiring writer Jamal Wallace (played by Rob Brown). This serves as a prompt to get the younger man to start writing his own words.

Writing prompts have been used by countless authors to overcome writer's block, with many successful authors dipping into this well of creativity to move past dry periods in their writing careers. In my experience, the more formal accountability programmes are the most beneficial. I have been a writing group member for the past few years. My writing has improved immeasurably from the ongoing support and regular prompts the group provides.

What is a Writing Prompt?

A prompt is a short piece of writing that acts as a springboard for an author's creativity, a starting point from which to begin writing.

I have created 30 writing prompts in this book for you to unlock your writing voice and build the habit of writing. You might choose to use one daily or weekly; whatever your schedule allows.

The important thing is to make a decision and stick to it. It is the discipline of writing to a schedule that will get your creative juices flowing. You have complete freedom to decide on the length of each piece, and of course, the direction you take.

Most of the prompts concern situations that professional people might encounter. This emphasis reflects the kinds of people I work with in my speaking community. And as a writing coach; people have a great deal of knowledge and insight, and the yearning to convey that knowledge through a book. A book acts as a legacy to our children and the world.

In many cases, the desire to write wells up from a deep sense of unease with one's current career and life focus. So many people feel trapped in a mental prison of their creation. They have built a once exciting career that now feels stale and unchallenging. Or it simply drives them too hard, so they have no time to nurture their wellspring of creativity. They're crying out for change.

Others want to expand their reach through writing and achieve greater impact in their field or discipline. A book achieves so much; the writing process revives the soul and the finished product can revive a career if the message is clear and authentic.

Try these prompts. Let your imagination flow. Writing prompts are just one of the arsenal of tools that have helped countless writers start or resume their writing journey, and they will help you too. In writing to a schedule, your creativity will begin to flow, and your unique voice will emerge – a voice you may have long suppressed.

How to make the most of this book

One of the greatest challenges of writing is the issue of self-doubt. I have faced it, sometimes in the form of Imposter Syndrome, which causes me to wonder what I am doing, and why. The result is that I either temporarily lose my voice, or bury it in a dry, dark cavern, as described in my Introduction. Self-doubt is a killer, and that's what we must silence – not our voice!

Here are some tips to make the most out of this book:

1. **Commit to writing every day:** Whether it's the first thing in the morning or during your lunch break, consistency is key to building a strong writing habit. Look at your lifestyle and find a slot where you can set aside time each day to follow the prompts.

2. **Try something different:** I designed each prompt to put you in the mindset of your character. Embrace the unknown and be fearless in exploring different mindsets. It will help you to connect with your readers.

3. **Connect with various emotions:** Emotions help your audience connect with your stories. I have added an "Emotional Word Wheel" to help you explore different feelings that you can add to your writing. There is more than one way to express a feeling, so make use of this valuable tool.

4. **Build your resilience by embracing writer's wellness:** Too many authors struggle with burnout. So, besides the prompts, this book includes sections on writers' wellness. Taking care of yourself (Physically, Mentally and Emotionally) will help you stick to your routine. Have a look at the three chapters dedicated to writing 'self-care'.

5. **Reflect and Revise:** After completing each prompt, take some time to go through what you have written. What emotions did it trigger in you? Does this help you connect with your potential readers? What challenges did you face? Use this feedback to revise and improve your work.

6. **Connect with other writers:** Writing can feel lonely, especially if you are new to writing, or struggling with writer's block. No one understands the writing process quite like another writer. Consider joining a writing community, or getting a book coach, where you can share your responses to the prompts and receive feedback from fellow writers. Reach out to me if you need a book coaching programme or need to join a writing community.

Unleash your creativity and dive into a fulfilling writing adventure using the tips, prompts, and wellness tools offered in this book. And remember, every word you write brings you one step closer to achieving your writing goals.

Escaping The Well of Silence

"And the vision that was planted in my brain still remains, within the sounds of silence."

Simon & Garfunkel

I REMEMBER THE DAY I led my voice through the garden of lies, intending to bury her. If I sit quietly, I can almost feel her hand in mine as I walked her down that path. She listened to my reasons why I could not let her speak. I was a master of logic. With each neatly wrapped excuse, she nodded in silence, drinking in the poison I had so beautifully packaged. My excuses had pushed her to the periphery of my life. My voice, my precious voice, had become an outcast, and here I was, planning to bury her. "It's just for a little while," I said.

I helped her down into the dry well. "You'll be safe here. I haven't forgotten you, I promise, and I'll be back soon to revive you. We'll achieve so much then."

Only months before, we had laughed under a waterfall of creativity. I had experienced the joy of working with her, the freedom and fulfilment I always felt when we worked in unison. She had brought comfort, too, when life got me down; her hand had gently soothed my brow, protecting my flickering light from the storm. No matter what I faced, she was there when I needed her.

Why did I not protect her as she had always protected me?

'Are you bringing the others?' she asked, as she stepped onto the tangled roots that lined the well.

"What others?" I asked.

'The other voices. The ones you guide and counsel? Can't you hear them?' Her words pierced my armour. I know that as I silence her, many other voices will be silenced, too. But I don't turn back. Instead, I make sure she climbs right down to the bottom of the dry cavern and place the cover firmly over the top. Swallowing back my tears, I know I am sacrificing her. But for what?

What a fraud I am. I have heard so many of the lies my clients tell me. The urgent investor meetings. The company embezzlement, the HR crisis, the wives who never spend time with them, the soccer matches, the award nominations, the dying parents. There is never enough time.

The excuses... they're all logical, true, and beautifully packaged parcels of poison. They keep so many voices cramped and half-formed. Why am I using the same excuses with my own voice? I have spent so much time whispering to souls, telling them that their voices matter, all the while watching as they drown or bury their voices. They dance with their own serpents, and I dance with mine. We all twist our bodies into more comfortable positions as we accommodate the ever tightening coils around our souls.

As I turn to leave, I see the other wells dotted throughout the garden, housing other voices that long to be free. They're all slightly different. Some are locked with ancient padlocks, rusted but holding strong. Discarded pages of half-written books surround others, fluttering in gusts of wind. Some are landscaped, with neat rows of flowers. There's an architectural masterpiece, covered in designer cladding. Stunning – but their beauty can never silence the whispering of the forgotten voices.

It is hard to tell where time begins and ends in this garden. The grains of sand trickle slowly. At some point, I turn to look back, and I see how much of the landscape is dotted with adorned wells. I notice the silence of the garden. Where are the birds? Where is the twittering, bustling, fertile ebb and flow of nature that would give life to this picture? I know if I go back to free my voice, I'll set it all in motion. I'll free my voice, and in so doing, I'll free the others, too, and who knows what the possibilities will be then?

I rush back to the well. How much time has passed, I do not know – and there she is, waiting to be let out. I reach for her, fighting off the screaming voices of my schedule. "No," I say, "Step back!" As my hand reaches down, she moves into the light, and I see her face. Gaunt, tear-streaked, but still alive. She stretches upward, like a child waiting to be lifted into its mother's arms.

"It's alright," I soothe. "I'm here now. I'm so sorry I left you!" As we embrace, I realise I am not the saviour here. Our embrace brings a surge of energy through my body, a sense of ease and of lightness. I feel whole again. How is it I never realised how much I needed her?

She has never needed me. It was always I, who needed her guidance, reassurance, strength and freedom. She is my steadfast companion, and

I will never let her go again. For I know now that I am nothing without the voice my Creator gifted me.

Day 1

"I can shake off everything as I write; my sorrows disappear, my courage is reborn."

Anne Frank

PETRA COULD FEEL THE sweat trickling down the sides of her cheeks, over her carefully applied blusher, and onto the collar of her white satin shirt.

It had been three years since her disgrace as a keynote speaker at the Global Speakers' Federation convention. If only she had declined that last shooter. If only she had; but her monumental failure was all history now. Petra had put it behind her. Having completed the 12 steps in her recovery programme, she felt ready for this moment, this chance to make it all right again.

There was only one person left on her list of people to make amends with. Thabo, her sponsor, squeezed her hand as he stood with her in the wings. "You've got this," he whispered. She squeezed back and, as the MC announced her name, she stepped out into the lights, smiling boldly.

Then her stomach lurched. There in the first row, she saw ...

Continue writing ...

Day 2

"Either write something worth reading or do something worth writing."

Benjamin Franklin

BOKANG GAZED OUT OVER the sea of angry faces, chanting and waving placards. Just one wrong word, and he knew that the tide could turn. This chanting mob could wreak havoc and endanger lives.

How was he going to tell husbands and fathers that the county's pandemic was about to strip them of their livelihoods? Destroy their dignity as primary breadwinners? Five thousand families would lose everything on this day. Five thousand ... the number the prophet had fed with five loaves.

But Bokang was no miracle worker. He was just a man dressed in a company golf shirt, black chinos, and standard-issue miner's safety boots with a neatly typed speech in his pocket. A speech he had practised in front of the mirror when his wife was asleep.

He found one face to focus on and stepped up onto the podium...

Continue writing ...

Day 3

"Let me live, love, and say it well in good sentences."

Sylvia Plath

LYNETTE SPENT THE MORNING, going through her growing list of unanswered emails. Over 2000 of them. She had tried to keep up, had tried all the productivity hacks. But the blasted inbox seemed to have a life of its own; growing overnight, it kept her on a constant treadmill of admin, requests, demands, and petty issues that robbed her of her sense of purpose. Today, she felt them like a python around her chest.

Delete, delete, delete ... She rolled her shoulders and pressed on the hard nodule that refused to release its grip on her muscles. In her dreams, Lynette was a world-famous speaker, but now ... she couldn't even afford a weekly head and shoulder massage. This volunteer work had her in its grip, and she felt drained.

Delete, delete, delete ... Mind-numbing, repetitive work, not the kind she believed would build a legacy for her family. And then she saw it. An email invitation that made her pause. That might change everything ...

Continue writing ...

Day 4

"I kept always two books in my pocket, one to read, one to write in."

Robert Louis Stevenson

FRIKKIE SQUEEZED THE BRIDGE of his nose just between his eyes. He knew the telltale early signs of a migraine. The 'Burnout Author," people called him. If he were not in so much pain, he would laugh at the hypocrisy of it all.

A burnout specialist who was himself in the early stages of the condition. It was humiliating! His carefully scheduled book tour, which initially coincided with his wife's final trimester, now clashed with their unexpected premature baby. Sleepless nights and irregular meals were throwing his entire plan out the window. It was a wonder that he had ever completed the editorial changes and gotten his book to the printer.

He was paying for it now. Exhaustion and a feeling of defeat washed over him as he listened to the host extolling his energy and the gifts he had to offer the world. The applause subsided, and the host turned to him with a smile.

All eyes were on Frikkie as they waited for him to respond ...

Continue writing ...

Day 5

"Writers live twice."

Natalie Goldberg

NTOMBI SAT IN THE white high-backed make-up chair and squinted under the lights.

"Are we nearly done?" she asked.

"Nearly. I just have to cover this mark," replied the make-up artist. Ntombi felt like a fool. She had noticed that her stilettos looked a bit lopsided before she left for the club two nights ago, but didn't want to change them. This was her monthly get-together with her girls and the opening night of an amazing new club. She had to look good.

The club's stainless steel decor and industrial-style staircase were the brainchild of the hottest new design talent in the country. She had been determined to get a selfie on opening night. But her stilettos did not care about Instagram selfies. Ntombi had tumbled down those stairs, parting ways with her shoes on the way down as her legs flew out, her arms flailed, and her skirt bunched up around her hips. Social media trolls had a field day with the pictures.

Today would be the first interview since that day and she was sure as hell not going to have her look ruined by a bruise. She was going to handle this with poise.

Suddenly ...

Continue writing ...

Day 6

"Tears are words that need to be written."

Paulo Coelho

WASEEM HAD NOT TOUCHED a single samoosa since his doctor showed his latest test results to his wife. But she was not here now, was she?

She was home in South Africa and he, attending a gathering of sales staff in India, was free. He felt like a naughty schoolboy who had run away from his parents at a festival. The event organiser had pre-ordered room service for him. There they lay in tantalising golden crispiness – six magnificent fiery vegetarian samoosas.

Waseem's mouth began to water before he reached for the first one. He moaned softly as he closed his eyes, savouring the first gratifying crunchiness of the deep-fried curried delight. Had he only known his wife was afraid of flying, he would have accepted these sales event invitations long ago.

Waseem lay on the bed in the hotel's terry robe in ecstasy. He reached for the second one, and the third. As he was about to bite into the fourth, a gut-wrenching pain exploded through his chest ...

Continue writing ...

Claim a Segment of Your Day

In the end, it's not the years in your life that count. It's the life in your years.

Abraham Lincoln

IMAGINE YOUR LIFE AS an orange. The outer part, the peel, is your protective layer, the casing that holds in all the goodness of the orange.

For many of us, the peel is our work. Without our work, we could not provide for our family, give them a home to live in, clothes to wear, and an education to sustain them.

As we peel away that outer layer, we find the juice of life. Our joy lies here. Each segment is an aspect of our lives that nourishes us and provides real sustenance to the ones we love. Each deserves attention because each is an essential element of the whole.

No one takes the time to peel an orange just for the sake of peeling it. That would be work without purpose. For most of us, we work to enjoy the fruit.

But a rare breed of people recognise that more than just yielding fruit, the purpose of the orange is to release the seed.

Even if you don't pick that orange or peel back the skin, nature will eventually erode the outer skin, dry out the juice, and release the seed. That is its true purpose.

Most of us throw away the seeds we find in our fruit. But inside them lie the potential of a thousand fruit trees.

What does the seed look like in your life? What experiences, what wisdom, what stories do you have?

Why not peel the orange, enjoy the fruit, and plant the seeds? Too difficult? Not at all! Perhaps you're deterred because you know you won't see the fruit of those seeds for years to come.

So you focus on the peel. At least we see a pay cheque at the end of the month when we focus on work, right? But our lives are so much more than the peel. We are the whole fruit, including the seeds.

Our seeds are the ideas we release into the world, expressed through deeds and words. Deeds pass away, but words written down live on long after we have gone. Ideas, expressed through words, change the world.

I know that years may pass before that seed fulfils its purpose. I also know that if I don't take the time to plant them, I am robbing the world of the beauty that those seeds can provide.

When you plan your day, let the first part be devoted to tending that seed.

Claim the first part of the day, for you and you alone. No emails or social media. Just a quiet time for you and your writing. As you begin to pay attention to what lies beneath the surface, you will discover the uniqueness of your voice, your wisdom, and your gift to the world.

Day 7

"The most valuable of all talents is that of never using two words when one will do."

Thomas Jefferson

"THERE ARE THREE THINGS you need to know about the Amazon that will keep you alive," Chuck grinned. He had given this speech so many times, that he knew it even better than the back of his sun-scorched, leathery hand. He was a wizened expert, respected for his years of intrepid traveling and adventures. People flocked to hear of his experiences. Chuck knew the pattern perfectly. He knew how to wrap an audience around his little finger, thrilling them with tales of his exploits.

The seasoned traveller leaned in closer – as if to share a well-guarded secret - and narrowed his eyes. "The first is ..."

The old adventurer stared at his outstretched index finger. "The first is ..."

All eyes were on Chuck as it dawned on him; He had completely forgotten his speech ...

Continue writing ...

Day 8

"To produce a mighty book, you must choose a mighty theme."

Herman Melville

"BRR, BRR." THABO'S PHONE vibrated in his pocket.

"Go away," he muttered under his breath. His PA had just returned from spiral binding the latest reports. How many more projections are they going to ask for? He thought back to the documentary he had watched about the ten most dangerous rivers in the world. The red-bellied piranhas of the Amazon could smell a drop of blood in 200 litres of water. That was what this felt like. Being in a river of blood-sucking capitalist piranhas with no mercy. They were wearing him down until his soul bled, and then they would go in for the kill.

He was exhausted. He had not slept well in weeks. He hadn't spent time with his family in months. Was this what he had studied for, what the world considered success? Out of the blue, an image flashed before him. A page of text, with his name at the top. It looked like the book he'd started writing years ago. A few pages, nothing more. The image pressed itself upon him, and he knew ...

Continue writing ...

Day 9

"Words are a lens to focus one's mind."

Ayn Rand

CHRISTINE HAD TO ADMIT she was an addict. Addicted to people pleasing. She had promised herself time and again that she would slow down, say no occasionally, and then found herself sucked in, yet again, to someone else's plan.

Her career, however illustrious, was seasoned with regret. Regret about what she had sacrificed to get here. She loved her job, her family, her friends, but enough was enough. Christine had embraced all that others expected of her for far too long, propelled by a constant sense that she was not enough. She had promised herself that she would make time to write, but hardly knew where to start. Every time she began to think more seriously about writing, something would come up. A family event, a tax audit, a talk. She was growing tired of pushing herself aside, waiting for that perfect month to write. When would it ever stop? Was there even such a thing as a perfect time?

"Do it!" she commanded herself. "Pick up a pen and start!" She picked up her notebook and pen. The first words appeared on the page.

Continue writing ...

Day 10

"A blank piece of paper is God's way of telling us how hard it is to be God."

Sidney Sheldon

Guo was staring at footage of another interview. Although the money that came with it was good – damn good! – he felt that there was no creativity in it. Before the pandemic, he had been making movies. But since no one could watch them, he started filming interviews instead. Surprisingly, even after the pandemic ended, he was still making them. It was an easy job. It had helped him survive the tough times, and keep the wolves from the door.

But now these were drying up too, and he'd already maxed out on his credit card. His wife kept pressing him to start writing again. But there was never enough time. Telling other people's stories is how he puts food on the table these days or has done for a few years. If that dried up, too, where would they be? He peered at the screen again. What was that in the background?

Guo zoomed in and saw ...

Continue writing ...

Day 11

"I love deadlines. I like the whooshing sound they make as they fly by."

Douglas Adams

PRETTY TURNED THE IGNITION. Another day taxi-ing her children around. She was a gifted writer, a loyal friend, and a slave to responsibility. No one seemed to understand. Pretty was sick of justifying herself to others. She had a gift, but children still had to be taken care of, and she wasn't about to neglect them just because she longed to write.

Why were people so quick to judge? Some of the mothers of her children's friends seemed to look down on her because she didn't have a high-flying career like they had, or claimed to have. Pretty was a writer! At least, she was when she had the time. She'd spent thousands of dollars on courses and hundreds of hours writing. "I'm a writer," she reminded herself, as she thought back to when she'd last spent time on her book. Was it this year, or the last? It was hard to recall.

"Mom," said her youngest, 'Why aren't we going?'...

Continue writing ...

Day 12

"One day I will find the right words, and they will be simple."

Jack Kerouac

PHILIP RAN HIS FINGERS through his hair. Another medical bill. Dear Lord, would it ever end? He had managed to get the first book out and, by all accounts, readers were loving it. But he needed money. Money to pay for promos. Money for extramurals and money for yet another medical bill. Was this what marriage was?

This did not feel like 'happily ever after'. This felt like being a frustrated bank manager, only without the perks. Clients were always complaining about not having enough, and blaming him for his lack of cooperation. Daddy bank – that's how they saw him.

What about his dreams? What about his books? Did marriage mean sacrificing your dreams - being stuck in a job where you are living from pay cheque to pay cheque? He shoved the bill into the bottom drawer. Let it wait. He had an event to go to, and he was sure as hell not going to tell the event coordinator that he did not have a free story for their delegates to download ...

Continue writing ...

Choose your Fuel

"Do the best you can until you know better. Then when you know better, do better."

Maya Angelou

We don't like to think of ourselves as machines, but in some ways, that's exactly what we are. Understanding how our bodies and brains work helps us to better manage our physical, mental, and spiritual mechanics. It is sad to think that people will buy an insurance plan for their car, use specific brands of polish or tyres, and yet pay so little attention to the engine that produces 100% of our income – our brains.

In the world of writing, you are an asset. Effective asset management in the manufacturing world considers the entire lifecycle of the equipment, parts, and production line. Managers make decisions on how to manage and service this equipment, to achieve what they call 'operative excellence'.

So what do asset management and operative excellence look like for the writer? Just as a well-maintained engine yields optimum output, our brains need to be at their optimal level to be creative. That is what any writer wants: a brain that can produce ideas that turn into books that delight, thrill, inform, comfort, and inspire readers. A poorly maintained brain (and body) will produce mediocre writing and take twice as long to do it.

Our brains and bodies are fuelled by glucose. While your body can store glucose, your brain cannot, so it needs a good-quality regular stream of glucose. Yes, the quality does matter.

Fuelling your body is not just about food. Lack of sleep and authors are old friends. When those deadlines are chasing you down, it becomes tempting to work longer hours than your mind and body can sustain. When the neurons in the brain become overworked, your thinking becomes impaired. You work, but you feel emotionally drained, which affects both your productivity and your creativity. This is why many authors simply can't imagine mustering the energy to write a second book.

In dealing with lack of sleep, many authors will tell you they live off coffee and, in some cases, chocolate. But these can make you irritable and jittery. Caffeine reduces hydration and can cause confusion, fatigue, and dizziness. These are complications that will hinder your book's

progress. Try to limit your coffee intake to a maximum of four cups a day.

Studies have shown that when companies adopt a healthy eating programme for employees, they get the following benefits for their workforce:

- increased cognitive function
- better concentration
- more energy and motivation
- decreased depression and anxiety
- heightened self-esteem

You may be writing alone, but that does not mean that you cannot learn and benefit from what large company-based studies have discovered. Simply by eating well and getting enough sleep, you can hugely boost your creativity and output.

Ultimately, if you want to earn from your books, you must approach your writing as a business and make the decisions that will enhance your fundamental equipment – your brain and body.

So, back to the coffee and chocolate. A high sugar intake, which is what we crave when our blood sugar drops, damages blood vessels in the brain that carry oxygen-rich blood. Long-term lack of oxygen in the brain can lead to vascular dementia. The result is poor reasoning, planning, judgment, and memory. Having dementia is hardly what a writer wants – in such a condition, you might not even remember your children, let alone leave a legacy for them.

On the other hand, too little blood sugar can make you dizzy, shaky, or irritable. When you are sitting writing for hours on end, this is a real risk. Sugary snacks and drinks, fast food, and processed foods don't provide the quality of nutrition to sustain you for long periods of writing.

Asset management requires planning. In the same way you would plan fuel stops for a long journey, you need to plan your brain's fuel intake.

Your brain takes up only 2% of your body weight, but consumes about 20% of your daily energy intake. It needs regular good quality fuel, so plan your healthy snacks and have them close to hand for a full day's work.

Fill up two, one-litre bottles of water and have them on your desk within easy reach. Or invest in a water dispenser or cooler. Water helps remove toxins from the brain and provides cushioning and lubrication for brain tissue. Every chemical reaction requires water, so when you are dehydrated, brain functioning is impaired.

Prepare a range of healthy snacks, such as fruit and nuts, and have them within easy reach of your computer or notebook.

Plan your lunch break. Too often we just grab whatever is in the refrigerator or call for takeaways, but if you plan your meals, you'll have more sustainable energy and your body and mind will thank you for it.

Here are a few healthy lunch options to consider preparing ahead of time:

- avocado and egg toast
- berry and spinach smoothie
- salmon salad with olive oil dressing
- chickpea tuna salad

- veggie and cream cheese sandwich

If you're writing in winter, cook up a big pot of soup the night before, and consume soup instead of coffee. Think about these on a cold winter's day:

- vegetable and turkey soup
- pumpkin spice butternut soup
- fish and vegetable soup
- chicken noodle soup
- beef and vegetable soup

While there has been heated debate about the benefits of supplementation, there are sufficient studies to convince me of the benefits of some supplementation options.

Omega-3 and Vitamin B are consistently found to be beneficial in various studies. Many individuals find that taking a high-quality multivitamin regularly has long-term benefits. It's advisable to research the best supplement for your body's needs. If you want to maximise your nutrient intake, consider having a blood test. Women, whose bodies tend to become iron-deficient quickly, may benefit from a simple combination of Vitamin C and iron.

Making sure you are fuelled for the mental, physical, and spiritual marathon that constitutes a book-writing project can go a long way to helping you create your legacy. Take care of the little things, the things you're probably thinking don't affect you much, and just see the difference it makes.

Now let's continue writing...

Day 13

"You never have to change anything you got up in the middle of the night to write."

Saul Bellow

CHOOSE A MELLOW MEDIUM-SIZED patterned saree for office use.' That is what the article said. Something that would 'not draw too much attention'. Fatima scoffed. Muted colours and patterns had not stopped the unwanted attention of that uncultured pig in finance. For too long Fatima had listened to the rumours, the whisperings from other women: 'Don't rock the boat. He is too powerful and will destroy your career.'

Just the thought of his leering look and his hand on her arm as she tried to discuss work-related matters made her feel sick. And she was not the only one. All the women in her department had received his unwanted attention.

Today she will be introducing him as the keynote speaker at their sales conference. Nobody knew it yet, but she planned to resign straight after the conference. Today she will speak the truth. What did she have to lose?

Fatima ran her fingers over the bold red and fuchsia fabric of her 'completely over-the-top' ceremonial saree. No more bland office clothing and bland office behaviour for her. Today, she will show that pig and the world who she really is ...

Continue writing ...

Day 14

"If my doctor told me I had only six minutes to live, I wouldn't brood. I'd type a little faster."

Isaac Asimov

RAKESH WENT OVER THE limousine checklist. The foam cannon he bought for the fleet he owned was well worth the investment. It saved the full-time car detailers multiple hours, allowing them to focus on the finer details. He checked the stock of Q-tips in the front to make sure the cup holders, crevices and vents could be cleaned before each customer entered a vehicle.

Rakesh's three-year-old chauffeur's uniform was in pristine condition. He adjusted his cap to the required angle. None of his staff knew he was the owner of the fleet, nor did any of his customers, from whom he especially wanted to conceal the truth. He checked the standard stock of 18-year-old Chivas Regal Gold Signature scotch whisky in the back of the vehicle. Its smooth taste helped to loosen the tongues of his high-flying exec clientele.

No one would expect a chauffeur to know anything about the

stock market. A misconception that had served him well over the past decade. From the small fortune he had accumulated by careful listening, he had bought this fleet. Rakesh was well on his way to building the palace of his dreams in the best part of the city.

Why, then, did he have this sense of unease in the pit of his stomach? He looked up from his checklist as the next customer arrived ...

Continue writing ...

Day 15

"We are all apprentices in a craft where no one ever becomes a master."

Ernest Hemingway

LERATO HAD MADE IT into the 20% of farmers who were female and landowners, but only just. Getting the land was one thing; now Lerato's challenge was not to become one of the hundreds of farmers who failed because they did not have the infrastructure for sustainable growth. Food security was a noble pursuit, but it was meaningless unless she could empower her workers to embrace her vision. A vision to swap to the high-value crops she knew could transform this little corner of the country.

Today Lerato would prove her mettle. She had drilled her workers for weeks, preparing them for questions the fresh produce buyers might have. The table was set for lunch and the best samples of her harvest were all laid out.

The farmer tucked her lavender blouse into her denim conti-suit pants and selected a pair of floral wellingtons to match. She took one last look at her welcome speech notes. The guests had arrived. It was showtime ...

Continue writing ...

Day 16

"If a nation loses its storytellers, it loses its childhood."

Peter Handke

LILIAN DUG HER FINGERNAILS into her palms. 'Left-over ladies'. The term was insulting. She had moved to this country to avoid the one-child policy of the country of her birth. But it seemed that the national mindset about women and ageing had followed her to her new home. Her doctorate made her seem old.' Like yellowed pearls', according to the article. Lilian glanced over again at the article she had torn from the magazine to fuel her resolve. She folded it neatly and placed it in her left breast pocket, close to her heart.

Today, she would address the press and potential investors. Her matchmaking agency targeted highly educated men and women looking for like-minded partners. It flew in the face of the traditional way of thinking; that only plain women needed an education. Not in her world, and certainly not in her company.

Lilian checked her lipstick, straightened her pencil skirt, and stepped onto the stage ...

Continue writing ...

Day 17

"For your born writer, nothing is so healing as the realization that he has come upon the right word."

Catherine Drinker Bowen

BENNY SIFTED THROUGH THE pile of documents his client had sent through. It was going to be a tough day. The team he was presenting to were mainly engineers and scientists turned sales consultants. This group of experts typically sat in front of their computers all day and seemed to expect customers to be impressed by their credentials. Credentials that did not automatically guarantee sales. These sales consultant's basic salaries were barely enough to cover a bond repayment for a one-bedroomed apartment; let alone clothe and feed a family.

Benny's experience with the unions gave him some advantage with tough negotiations. But getting a demoralised group of raw 'salespeople' to 'up their game' is a tough call.

A member of this team who hadn't paid his home loan in two months was on the brink of signing a life-changing deal. However, rumour had it that the CEO of the client company usually stonewalled projects over $3 million, and the deal might not go through. "How do you motivate a man whose hope was hanging by a thread?" thought Benny.

He knew the deal was a good one, but the consultant was too inexperienced and probably too desperate to close the deal. And that was just one team member. There they sat, each desperate in their way, waiting to receive something – anything that would change their prospects. Benny pushed open the glass door...

Continue writing ...

Day 18

"Write. Rewrite. When not writing or rewriting, read. I know of no shortcuts."

Larry L. King

ANELE STEPPED INTO THE class. Her baby sister had not stopped crying the entire night, and she was exhausted. Her mother's employer had told her if she missed another day of work, she should not bother coming back. Anele knew what that meant. More work for her. The next time the baby fell sick, she'd have to take her to the clinic.

When would she ever have time for schoolwork? The oral she was presenting today had the potential to be good. She knew it, but she'd barely had time to prepare. Yesterday, after picking up the baby from daycare, washing all the clothes, and cooking dinner, she'd had exactly an hour to polish the speech. It wasn't enough time.

Sometimes she wished she could run away. None of her classmates seemed to have her responsibilities. Their Facebook pages were full of parties, fun, and pouting. She spent her weekends trying to keep the baby happy and her mother from despairing.

Last month, someone sponsored her class to go to a Youth Speaking Summit. Anele had felt inspired, yet today all that inspiration had evaporated. She looked down at her grubby prep notes, smeared with baby porridge. The exhausted schoolgirl dreaded even the thought of standing up in front of the class.

And then an idea came to her, something she'd heard at the Summit: *'Your pain is your positioning!'*

Continue writing ...

Create Your Space

"I don't know whether nice people tend to grow roses or growing roses makes people nice."

Roland A. Browne

FEW THINGS WILL GIVE you the emotional highs and lows of a writing project. One moment you're an invisible creator of worlds, racing along like a river in full flow; the next moment you're a blubbering idiot who can't string two sentences together. That's why, as writers, we need to invest in a writing space that supports our process.

Having a designated writing space can help programme your mind to function better. You will begin to associate that space with productive work. Your environment affects your mind, so take the time to create the kind of space that warms your heart. A space that feeds your soul, is comfortable, and yet geared toward work. Then set some ground rules for members of your family so they know that when you're in your writing space, you are *working*.

What do you need in that space? Something beautiful to inspire you – maybe a view from a window that soothes your soul, or a painting on the wall, or an object you enjoy resting your eyes on. Then, the practicalities: Your Rocketbook, notepad, tablet, or computer, whichever tool works best for you. Possibly some large sheets of paper and coloured pens for mind mapping. If you're writing a murder mystery, have a pin board to replicate the mind maps that TV detectives use to show the relationships between the characters they're dealing with. Don't forget space for your snacks and water. Once you have your items in place, remove everything else, so you have a clean and clutter-free surface to work on.

If you can't find a space at home, you can escape to your favourite coffee shop and write there . Many coffee shops love to have their resident author grace their environment, knowing they are inspiring something wonderful. In this case, make sure you have a backpack, pre-packed with all your writing bits and pieces so that you can just get on with it.

If you're at home, find something that will signal it is your writing time. I have a writing mug with my company logo on it that says, 'I can see no greater honour to our Creator than to paint the picture He planted in your heart with your words.' When my children see that on the edge of my desk, they know I am not to be disturbed.

There are also some comfort issues to consider. You're going to be sitting for quite some time, so get the best office chair you can afford. When Jerry Jenkins, 21-time New York Times bestselling author, started writing, he wrote sitting on a couch with a plank on two kitchen chairs as a desk. You don't need an expensive chair to start, but over time, poor spine protection will take its toll, so start saving up for a decent chair.

Sitting for long periods in a chair with poor back support increases stress on the lumbosacral vertebrae (the part of the spine that supports the majority of the body's weight and protects the primary nerves that arise from the spinal cord). This increased stress results in pain in the lower back. Good lumbar support keeps your spine aligned in its natural elongated 'S' shape.

It always amazes me that people will spend thousands of dollars on a television, but won't invest in their spinal health. After two bouts of whiplash and prolonged neck challenges, I know first-hand how musculoskeletal pain can disrupt my writing process.

When you hunch over a computer for hours, your spine adopts a 'C' shape that can lead to backache, neck pain, tension headaches, sciatic nerve pain, and impaired breathing caused by compression of the lungs. Compression of the lungs restricts blood flow to your vital organs, specifically your brain, resulting in fatigue and poor concentration. These are not things that you want as a writer. Your goal is to remain comfortable for as long as possible. So if you haven't yet found the perfect chair for you, invest in a lumbar support cushion to properly align your muscles and spine.

An additional layer of comfort is a footrest. If you are short, as I am, this is essential. Footrests align posture, reduce fatigue, and ease pain in the feet, ankles, knees and thighs.

The worst time for writing for me is undoubtedly winter. I tend to write from 04H00 until 07H00, and in winter, that can be excruciating. So I have a fleece blanket hanging on a hook in the office and I always cover my legs and feet. I also have my favourite comfortable fleece jacket close by and some cut-off gloves to keep warm without the use of dehydrating artificial heat. If it is particularly cold, I will put a hot water bottle under my feet as this warms me all over. Owning a high-quality flask that keeps water hot for hours prevents me from constantly having to get up to boil water. This keeps me focused.

Creating a writing space is not just about the physical attributes of your environment. It includes the mental space. It took me time, but my children have come to respect the words, 'Mommy is writing.' This means they close the door, keep the TV in the next room low and generally avoid coming into the office.

If your environment is particularly noisy or you have neighbours who have a construction project on the go, you might want to invest in noise-reducing headphones.

A vision board has helped, too. I am a great believer in surrounding myself with words and images that work subtly on my mind, edging me toward my goals every time I dwell on them.

Getting your space ready for writing may seem like a lot of effort, but once it's set up, you'll reap the rewards in creativity and that marvellous state known as 'flow'.

Now let's get back to writing...

____

____

____

____

____

Day 19

"Style means the right word. The rest matters little."

Jules Renard

Bongani raked the leaves in his garden meditatively. They reminded him of the scattered thoughts littering his conscious mind. On cool autumn mornings, he would often stand on the terrace, coffee in hand, and survey the random colourful pattern across his lawn.

During the raking, now and then, he would find one green leaf that seemed to have fallen from the tree. Perhaps a bird had been pecking at it, or part of the stem was weaker than the rest. But there it was, a splash of green amongst a sea of brown and golden leaves. He needed only one fresh idea. One thought with which he could transform a client's process. That master idea he could run with. An evergreen concept that could be crafted into a keynote, a workshop, and an online course.

Most of his friends employed gardeners. They said they had worked hard enough to get to where they wanted to be and weren't about to spend Saturdays cleaning their own yards. They laughed at him when he said he couldn't join them on Saturday afternoons. "Find someone else to do your manual labour!" they chorussed.

Bongani scoffed at the notion. There was no way he was hiring a gardener. This was his time. No kids demanding his attention. His wife was at the gym with her friends. It was just Bongani in the solitude of his garden. It was his time to think, his time to process, to create.

And then he found it. His next idea ...

Continue writing ...

Day 20

"The first sentence can't be written until the final sentence is written."

Joyce Carol Oates

KIRAN THREW BACK A handful of anti-inflammatories. Her hip ached as if her grandson had thrown a fastball made of iron directly at her. Kiran's 'at any cost' attitude had gotten her out of her original garage office and into the top seat of her own multi-national company. But it did not stop the physical pain gnawing at her sanity.

Voted one of the most powerful women on the planet, she felt far from powerful now. She remembered her mother's agonising death after an undetected fracture. Kiran had promised herself this would never happen to her. But all those endless nights huddled over her computer had taken their toll.

Kiran had postponed her appointment with the orthopaedic surgeon so many times that the best she could get was six months from now. Could she endure the pain until then? It was so bad that her husband had moved into the spare room two months ago, as every movement of his body sent jolts of pain through hers. He never complained, but she could feel the distance growing between them.

The powerhouse CEO picked up her notes for her keynote on empowerment and what it meant to her.

She winced as she took the first step onto the stage. Kiran looked at the sea of faces, threw her notes in the air, and started the speech she had never dared to write ...

Continue writing ...

Day 21

"I don't need an alarm clock. My ideas wake me."

Ray Bradbury

WENDY SLIPPED INTO HER designer overalls. If she is to be stuck in a man's world, she is going to look good in it. None of those crazy pants that were not designed for authentic women with real curves. Her assistant announced that the photographer had arrived and that the 140 GC Motor Grader was ready.

Wendy was no poser. She was going to take that photographer on a ride that would prove she was not just a pretty face. She was the real deal, a woman who walked her talk. This yellow baby grader weighs 14,310 kg, and when that photographer sees her driving it, he will know just who he is dealing with.

The 5.2-foot woman was tired of those foul-mouthed, testosterone-pumped men talking down to her. She was in charge now. Wendy hauled herself into the driver's seat and beckoned to the photographer.

"Come on, honey, jump up! You're going to have the ride of your life," she grinned ...

Continue writing ...

Day 22

"It's none of their business that you have to learn to write. Let them think you were born that way."

Ernest Hemingway

KAMOGELO RUBBED HIS KNEE and stared at the WhatsApp notification.

How could he have been such an idiot? That soccer scholarship had been his and Palesa's ticket out of there. His coach had warned him about running onto the field without warming up. But Palesa had persuaded him to take her clubbing the night before his debut match in the new team, and now he had busted his knee. To top it all, Palesa dumped him soon afterward. For months, he had blamed her. It was her fault his knee was in this state. How could she have dumped him when he was down? Why had she ruined his life in this way?

His friend Jabu had given him a good kick up the attitude. "Man, I would have dumped your sorry butt long ago. You could have manned up and told Palesa, 'No, baby, I am building our lives here. Let me go out and do my thing in top form.' She never forced you. You just didn't believe in your goals enough to sacrifice for them."

Kamogelo knew Jabu was right. He was 100% to blame for his troubles. The fallen soccer player opened the message again. It was from Jabu, and it pulled no punches. "Face it, bud, your sporting career is over. Have you thought about ...?"

Continue writing ...

Day 23

"When I say work, I only mean writing. Everything else is just odd jobs."

Margaret Laurence

DOROTHY'S INTERNAL ALARM CLOCK yanked her from sleep at 04:26. Come rain or shine, sickness or health, this clock was relentless.

She had trudged through three meetings the preceding day. Her only reprieve was sitting on the couch watching a movie. Hardly relaxing though. The movie was two hours of unrelenting warfare, prescribed for her by her mentor as research for her book. Armed with three pages of notes for her follow-up meeting, she had finally allowed herself to slip under the covers at 23H00. But now it was showtime again. People thought being an entrepreneur was a life of freedom. But there are no sick days for those who work for themselves and are trying to write a book at the same time.

Dorothy had three clients' work to get out, with all their deadlines falling on the same day. Plus homework for her speaking class. She had also promised herself to get one more chapter written, before the end of the week. She must have been mad. How would she ever juggle this lot?

Opening her email account, Dorothy saw a message that made her heart leap ...

Continue writing ...

Day 24

"I almost always urge people to write in the first person. ... Writing is an act of ego and you might as well admit it."

William Zinsser

"I AM TIRED OF you sitting on your butt," his sales manager had told him.

Lance was not lazy. Give him a task and he will give it his all. But taking initiative when he was fearful, was another matter altogether. How could a man with a family to feed admit that he was just too scared to take the next step? What if he gave it his all, and still failed? Lance knew he stood to lose so much.

It was easier to keep busy, and never think about the big change needed. Just plug away at his job the way it is now, and do his best to get some enjoyment from life. Not easy. Constant power outages. Martha's constant nagging. The kids' endless demands. There was not much time on weekends after mowing the lawn and seeing to the chores forced on him. Alone with his earphones, watching Netflix, was his only form of stress relief.

Saturday afternoon. He settled down with the remote, snacks at hand. He was about to press play when his phone pinged. A message from his boss. This was unusual. Should he ignore it? Tempting. But he couldn't resist. He picked up his phone and read.

"Lance, you won't believe it," the message started ...

Continue writing ...

Choose your Destination

"Your vision will become clear only when you can look into your own heart. Who looks outside, dreams; who looks inside, awakes."

Carl Jung

I MENTIONED A VISION board. This, and vision in general – is something most schools don't teach us. Schools programme us to get an assignment or a test out of the way so we can move on to the next task. If you don't finish on time, you're penalised, and if you do finish on time, you're quickly ushered into the next task. Education is designed that way because schools were created during the Industrial Revolution when factories needed large numbers of orderly, compliant people.

You and I still have traces of our school programming embedded in us. At school we learned structure and discipline, which are certainly valuable and stand us in good stead throughout life. But we need something more than discipline; we need *vision*. If you spend any time in a corporation, your vision is shaped by the leadership of that organisation. How about the vision for your book?

The Cheshire Cat, in the book *Alice's Adventures in Wonderland* by Lewis Carroll, said: 'If you don't know where you are going, any road will get you there.' He was describing the absurd world of Wonderland, where it hardly mattered which direction you walked in because you would certainly end up somewhere. That's hardly our goal as authors or as human beings. We want to end up somewhere good!

That's why I always ask new authors what their vision is for their book. Most people say, 'I want to write a bestseller.' Now, as a publisher, I know that in certain markets, and with a highly funded promo campaign, you can get to best-seller status quite easily – especially with the many, many Amazon Best Seller categories – and then in just 30 minutes, someone else's book can replace yours.

Shouldn't our real goal be to make an impact? That is my vision. Impact can vary; for instance, you might have a fleeting impact on 1 000 readers who soon forget you, or a massive impact on 100 who become devoted fans and want to buy whatever you write in the future. You'd have to decide which you value most.

Remember that in the world of non-fiction, most books are written to *try to solve a problem*. In my book coaching program, I press new authors for details to help hone their vision. I ask questions like:

- Who is the ideal reader?
- What lifestyle does that reader have?
- What problem do they have?
- And, most importantly, how are you going to solve that

problem for them?

Once you understand this, you have a point of departure. Many successful people attribute their success to one or two events that formed a turning point in their lives. A word from a teacher, a rousing speech, perhaps a friend's accident. For many people, it was a reading book.

This could be your book. And after all the effort you put into your book, you want it to make an impact; preferably on many people, not just a handful.

If that is your 'destination', the burning question is: What steps do you need to take to get there?

You, dear reader and future author, have a gift in your heart. One that can transform the hearts and minds of the many who need to hear your message.

Begin with the end in mind. Work through your goals in writing your book, from the one great overarching goal to the smaller goals along the way. Get your space organised, then liberate your mind from the strictures that have held you back.

You have it in you. Now get your book out there, attract and retain readers, and build your lasting legacy.

If you need help along the way, look out for my book **"What Would a Succesful Author Do?"**

Now lets get back to writing...

Day 25

"When writing a novel a writer should create living people; people, not characters. A character is a caricature."

Ernest Hemingway

VANITHA PICKED UP THE magazine. Another PR photo shoot and another accolade.

She watched little Kash pressing his chubby fingers into the porridge bowl. His face was a work of art fashioned from teething drool and porridge. He was her jewel, her delight. Her first grandbaby. She could just kiss his chubby little cheeks forever. But shareholders' demands would not wait.

Vanitha had fought so hard to get to the top and sacrificed so much. Other grandmothers were enjoying retirement. They had rooms or apartments in their children's homes and unrestricted access to their grandchildren. Part of her yearned for that. But honestly, she liked what she had, too. The power, the influence she wielded. Men listened attentively when she spoke. Vanitha had everything so many women dreamed of. Was it all still worth it when baby Kash was growing up so fast? When would she say 'enough' to the jam-packed days and late nights, and take the time to enjoy her grandchild and others still to come?

The agenda for the next board meeting was in her inbox, waiting for her to make amendments. There was only one amendment she could think of ...

Continue writing ...

Day 26

"I will defend the importance of bedtime stories to my last gasp."

J. K. Rowling

Palesa's pink pout filled the screen as she kissed the camera in preparation for her next TikTok video. Her mother had complained again about her going out in a micro-mini. But didn't her mother parade herself in the Reed Dance when she was a girl? Palesa didn't see any knee-length skirts in those dances. Maybe marriage just made you old and a prude.

"Those dances are part of a ceremony that promotes purity before marriage," her mother had argued. "At least don't post where you work or where you get your taxi." Palesa shook her head and checked her followers and likes. She was making it. Just a few more and she could monetise. Then the sky was the limit.

Influencers made big bucks, and she wanted in on it. She had already planned on everything she would buy when the money started to roll in. Palesa checked her outfit and was about to hit 'record' when she heard a crash and a wail. She ran to the kitchen where her mother stood, her face an expression of dismay. Her teacup lay shattered on the floor.

Palesa pulled the phone from her mother's hand and read the message. Her cousin Mpho, a fellow TikTok user, had been ambushed while waiting for public transport. A crowd had ...

Continue writing ...

Day 27

"If one is lucky, a solitary fantasy can totally transform one million realities."

Maya Angelou

MANDLA'S NAME MEANT STRENGTH, but he felt far from strong at this moment. His client market was so diverse. He claimed to be a 'selling to millennials expert', which implied that he understood the different generations' buying styles. Millennials, he understood. Mandla used their language and technology with ease in the punchy articles he wrote to boost brands, but it was the baby boomers who ran this company. They were alien to him.

How was he going to sell his style of consulting to someone who looked like a contemporary of his grandfather? A man who seemed proud of the fact that he wasn't on social media? Mandla resisted the urge to fidget with his portfolio bag of storyboards as he sat under the grim stare of the ancient-looking receptionist. The door opened...

Continue writing ...

Day 28

"Vulnerability is our most accurate measurement of courage."

Brene Brown

SHIKHA PINNED HER HAIR back and eyed the sensible court shoes neatly laid out beneath a row of suits in her walk-in closet. Her wardrobe consultant had advised sneakers and more relaxed outfits. They'd certainly be a lot more comfortable than the court shoes and dark suits she wore daily.

But women of her age and status did not wear sneakers to the boardroom – did they? Test groups about the company; which invariably reflected opinions about the CEO, had come back with an 'out of touch' and 'dated' response. Her consultant had advised Shikha to update herself, starting with her look. She was all for stepping out of your comfort zone to facilitate growth, but the new look of casual shoes, shirts hanging out and open necklines; seemed too foreign to adopt. The CEO winced when she thought of her new consultant's parting words.

"Really, Shikha. Why do you even pay me if you don't accept any of the suggestions I make?"

She picked up the discarded storyboards and looked through the ideas again. What was this woman thinking? One of the outfits showed …

Continue writing …

Day 29

"Tall oaks from little acorns grow."

Andrew Carnegie

ELIZABETH HAD WORKED HER tail off in every single setting. At school, she'd excelled. Her peers had voted her the most likely to succeed in everything she would ever do. But somehow, Elizabeth had stopped short of reaching the level she knew she was capable of. Just as things start getting really exciting, she'd miss a meeting or change the direction of a project, and then the expected trajectory would nose-dive.

Her dream team told her it was classic Imposter Syndrome. She was self-sabotaging, and she knew it. Elizabeth felt powerless to change it. Just that week, one of her friends had asked why she did not share her appearance on a prestigious podcast with her professional community. If she was honest, she was happier seeing others succeed than herself. If she climbed too high, she'd have a reputation to uphold, and how would she handle the pressure, then?

But something had to change. Women far younger than her were exceeding her accomplishments and seemed comfortable in their roles.

Why didn't she? How could she possibly lead a team authentically if she kept holding herself back?

Elizabeth looked at the new list of podcasts her consultant had sent through and knew that today was the day. She had to apply to at least one of them ...

Continue writing ...

Day 30

"My powers are ordinary. Only my application brings me success."

Isaac Newton

BERTUS WAS TIRED OF the online dating scene. He had made his first million before the age of 25, but it left little time to find that elusive soulmate. He had spent every waking hour building his business, and now it was time to settle down and start a family. But the mindless conversations with gold diggers made him want to run back to the farm and wear khaki for the rest of his days.

Maybe these guys who ordered brides off the internet were on to something, he mused. Why was it so hard to find an intelligent woman who worked hard for her own money? One who still believed in the traditional values of family, responsibility, and quiet nights at home with a home-cooked dinner? Heck, she didn't even have to cook the dinner.

He'd tried pretending he was poor, but that hadn't attracted what he was looking for either. And some of the more wealthy women made him feel like a gawking teenage boy. Couldn't a woman combine success with just ... being normal? Or was it just him that was the problem? He could address a room full of venture capitalists, but seemed unable to get past a second date.

Bertus looked at the profile print of the woman who was to be his next date. She wasn't bad-looking and worked as a forensic entomologist. Bertus wasn't quite sure what that was, but decided to take the plunge.

'Hey, Wilhelmina,' he began ...

Continue writing ...

A Word From The Author

I AM KIM VERMAAK, a South African author, speaker, trainer, coach and publisher who has been helping authors, entrepreneurs and knowledge workers build their brands for over 20 years. I have a passion for bringing wisdom into the art of storytelling, and have been told that I've touched the hearts of many with my medieval fantasy series involving the eternal battle between good and evil. I love empowering aspiring authors to turn their own dreams into reality.

My superpower is turning crushing events into victories, not only in my own life, but in the lives of others. I have helped, and continue to help, aspiring authors find their voices, unlock their stories and hone their unique message to the world through well-crafted fiction and non-fiction manuscripts. I see writing as the perfect combination of truth telling, creativity and entrepreneurship, and revel in each aspect.

I hope I can help you. Whether you're an aspiring author or a brand manager, you deal in ideas, and ideas transform the world. The key is to be authentically *you*. As the opening scene of this book suggests, the writer's first job is to find their voice – thereafter, the magic can start to happen.

Extract From My Next Book

WHAT WOULD A
SUCCESSFUL
AUTHOR
DO?

THE POWER OF THE
READER MAGNET

K. VERMAAK

Introduction

"Dreams don't work unless you do."

John C. Maxwell

Do you have "Write a Book" on your bucket list? Do you have a friend who wants to write a book? Let's take this thought process a little further. Do you want to earn a living from your books? Now that is a worthy dream, but sadly one that many won't achieve. Why? Because most people don't take action. They may make some sort of show of activity. But are they taking deliberate steps towards their goal? By buying this book, you took a deliberate step. Now let me ask you this:

"What are you doing today to make your dreams a reality?"

For most author dreamers, that manuscript remains hidden in their mind, or worse, in their bottom drawer. I say worse because being in the bottom drawer means they had the courage to start, but never finished.

In the movie Knight and Day, Roy Miller (played by Tom Cruise) tells June Havens (played by Cameron Diaz), a classic car restorer; that "Someday - is code for never." June shared her dream of "someday" driving cross-country in a 1966 Pontiac GTO that she inherited from her father. When Roy Miller meets her, she has just purchased the parts needed to restore the car so that she can give it to her sister as a wedding gift.

Wait... for her sister? How does this align with June's dream, or her sister's dream? In short, it does not. The idea seems laughable, but that is what the average author does with their time. They exchange it for someone else's dream. Having been in that place, I agree with Roy Miller.

'Someday' Is code for 'never'.

...Unless you take action!

If you don't have a detailed plan to reach your author-dream with solid deadlines, your dream will die with you. The "What Would a Successful Author Do Series" is dedicated to helping authors take action in key areas that will help boost their focus on stepping into action to change the direction of their careers.

The philosophy of **"Be - Do - Have"** is that first, you have to **"BE"** the person you aspire to be. Then you have to "**DO"** the things that a successful person in your chosen field/career would do. Only then will you **"HAVE"** what a successful person in that industry has.

While many people crave having what success brings, few people will do the activities that successful people have disciplined themselves to do, on a daily basis.

In this book we will delve into a fundamental part of selling for authors. That is, to find readers and tempt them to test your brand, and then commit to your brand.

One of the key components to do this, is the READER MAGNET.

Other Books By The Author

NON FICTION

Time in a Bottle: Writing Your Legacy

What Would a Successful Author Do? The Power of Reader Magnets

FICTION

Novellas

A Mother's Warning

Curse of the Dragons

Guides

The Dragon Whisperer Field Guide

Novels

(The Chronicles of Nadine)

The Last of the Silver Wings

The Fire Within The Storm

The Call of the Ancients

The Tears of the Crystal Heart

Short Stories

The Fallen's Second Chance

Just The Right Amount of Spice

The Guarded Heart

www.ingramcontent.com/pod-product-compliance
Lightning Source LLC
Chambersburg PA
CBHW071221090426
42736CB00014B/2917

* 9 7 8 0 7 9 6 1 1 6 7 1 0 *